FEAR THIS BOOK

Your Guide to
Fright, Horror, &
Things That Go Bump in the Night

written by
JEFF SZPIRGLAS

illustrated by
RAMÓN PÉREZ

PORTER MEMORIAL BRANCH LIBRARY
NEWTON COUNTY LIBRARY SYSTEM
6191 HIGHWAY 212
COVINGTON, GA 30016

MAPLE
TREE
PRESS

Maple Tree Press Inc.
51 Front Street East, Suite 200, Toronto, Ontario M5E 1B3
www.mapletreepress.com

Text © 2006 Jeff Szpirglas
Illustrations © 2006 Ramón Pérez

All rights reserved. No part of this book may be reproduced or copied in any form without written consent from the publisher.

Distributed in Canada by Raincoast Books
9050 Shaughnessy Street, Vancouver, British Columbia V6P 6E5

Distributed in the United States by Publishers Group West
1700 Fourth Street, Berkeley, California 94710

Cataloguing in Publication Data
Szpirglas, Jeff
    Fear this book : your guide to fright, horror, and things that go bump in the night / written by Jeff Szpirglas ; illustrated by Ramón Pérez.

Includes index.
ISBN-13: 978-1-897066-66-9 (bound) ISBN-10: 1-897066-66-X (bound)
ISBN-13: 978-1-897066-67-6 (pbk.)   ISBN-10: 1-897066-67-8 (pbk.)

    1. Fear—Juvenile literature. I. Pérez, Ramón II. Title.

BF575.F2S96 2006   j152.4'6   C2006-900315-7

Design & art direction: Claudia Dávila
Illustrations: Ramón Pérez

We acknowledge the financial support of the Canada Council for the Arts, the Ontario Arts Council, the Government of Canada through the Book Publishing Industry Development Program (BPIDP), and the Government of Ontario through the Ontario Media Development Corporation's Book Initiative for our publishing activities.

ONTARIO ARTS COUNCIL
CONSEIL DES ARTS DE L'ONTARIO

Printed in China

A   B   C   D   E   F

Acknowledgments
Writing a book like this one means consulting a number of other sources: books, magazines, journals, and the Internet. Equally important are the experts in the field who have helped check the facts in this book. I'm eternally grateful for the help of **David Moscovitch**, Ph.D., a good friend and a good clinical psychologist. Put your hands together for a big round of applause for the following: Paul Adams (www.harryprice.co.uk); D. L. Ashliman, Ph. D., University of Pittsburgh; Tavis J. Basford, MD; Randolph Blake, Psychology Department, Vanderbilt University; Richard B. Borgens, Ph.D., Purdue University; Dr. Louis E. Catron, Professor of Theater, College of William and Mary; Denise Chen, Ph.D., Psychology Department, Rice University; Dr. Valerie Curtis, London School of Hygiene and Tropical Medicine; Graham C.L. Davey, Ph.D., University of Sussex; Beatrice de Gelder, Ph.D., Harvard Medical School; Matthew H. Edney, History of Cartography Project, University of Wisconsin; Paul Ekman, Ph.D., author, *Emotions Revealed*; Greg Febbraro, Ph.D., Department of Psychology, Drake University; M. Brock Fenton, Ph.D., Department of Biology, The University of Western Ontario; Thomas J. Fernsler ("Dr. 13"), University of Delaware; Andrew Fox, Fox Shark Research Foundation; Dean Glass, Save Our Heritage Organisation; Richard J. Hand, University of Glamorgan; Sherrill Harbison, Ph.D., University of Massachusetts Amherst; Lynne A. Isbell, Ph.D., Department of Anthropology, University of California; Paul Karoly, Ph.D., Department of Psychology, Arizona State University; Sally L.D. Katary, Ph.D., Department of Classical Studies, Thorneloe University; Prof. Joe Kunkel, University of Massachusetts Amherst; Steve Lee, HollywoodLostAndFound.net; Professor Ronald J. Leprohon, University of Toronto; Dr. Richard Lord, National Physical Laboratory; Vera Micznik, Ph.D., University of British Columbia; Joel Marks, Professor of Philosophy, University of New Haven; Dr. Elizabeth Miller (www.blooferland.com); Antónia Monteiro, Ph.D., Department of Ecology and Evolutionary Biology, Yale University; Daniel A. Nathan, Ph.D., Department of American Studies, Skidmore College; Arne Öhman, Ph.D., Department of Clinical Neuroscience, Karolinska Institutet; Thomas H. Ollendick, Ph.D., Department of Psychology, Virginia Polytechnic Institute and State University; Marion Preest, Ph.D., The Claremont Colleges; Paul Rozin, Ph.D., Department of Psychology, University of Pennsylvania; Reg Ryan, Monte Cristo Homestead; Dr. Murray B. Stein, Department of Psychiatry, University of California; Rick C. West (www.birdspiders.com); Izak Westgate, Hockey Hall of Fame; Paul J. Whalen, Ph.D., Dartmouth College; Richard Wiseman, Ph.D., Psychology Department, University of Hertfordshire; John Yeomans, Ph.D., Department of Psychology, University of Toronto. A very special thanks to my uncle Larry, who told me what a soffit is.

CONTENTS

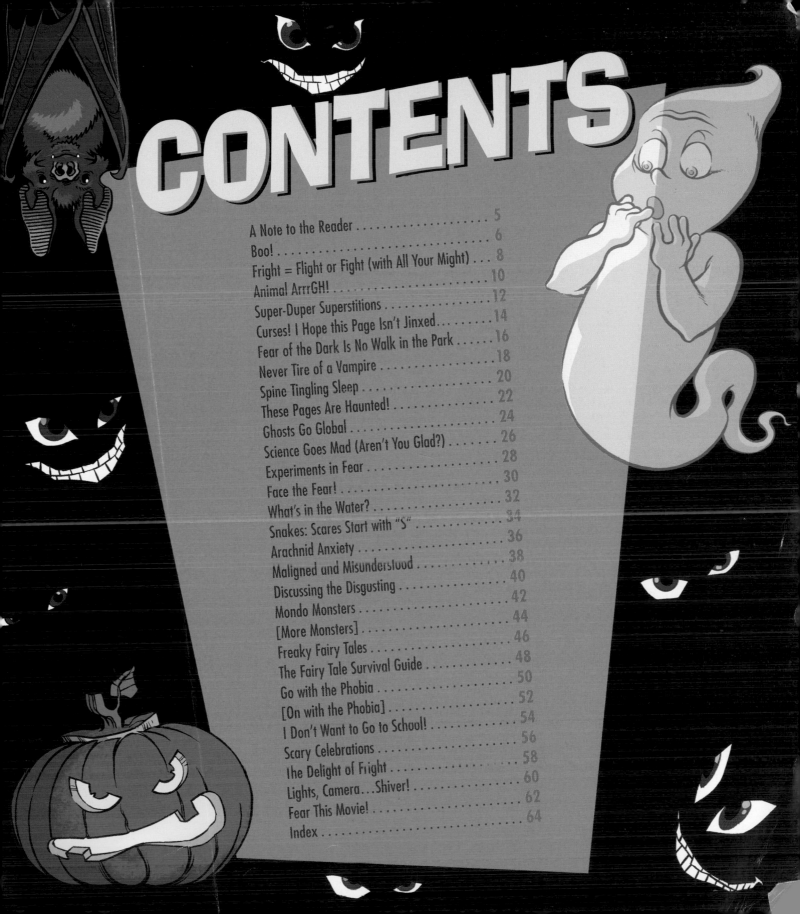

A Note to the Reader

"Don't do it," my mother implored me. "You'll be scared!" Ah, but I was young and brave and more than a little foolish.

"Yes," I told myself, "I *will* watch *Jaws 2*. And I will *not* be scared."

The horror movie about a shark terrorizing a beach resort was playing on TV. My parents had left a babysitter to watch over me. The babysitter had no problem with *Jaws 2*, and neither did I. Until I saw **The Scene**: a pair of teenagers on a sailboat were attacked by a hungry great white shark. The boy fell overboard as the boat was dragged across the choppy ocean. His girlfriend screamed for him to swim quickly. She could see the dorsal fin of the shark grow closer, and closer, until....

…Until the boy was dragged under the water, which ran red with blood.

I did not fall asleep easily that night, and when I did, I awoke with nightmares. My experience with the movie left me nervous of the open water and terrified of sharks. But there was still hope. Bit by bit, I allowed myself to flip open old issues of *National Geographic* magazine to stare at pictures of sharks. As I learned more about sharks, I began to appreciate what efficient hunters they are. They've been around for nearly 400 million years, and have changed little for over 100 million years. What marvelous creatures.

We all have fears. Some we have by the time we're born. Others we learn over time or develop from a scary experience. This book is full of the things you may fear: ghosts, snakes, spiders, heights, monsters, school, and more. You might not like these things, but the more you know about them, the less you may fear them.

Brace yourself. Hold someone's hand for comfort if you need to. When you're ready, take your finger and turn the page. But don't say I didn't warn you....

Jeff

WITHDRAWN

BOO!

How's your heart? Pumping blood a mile a minute? Did you throw the book down in terror at the sight of this page? Are you only now reading these words after shakily retrieving your book from the floor? Startles are often associated with fear, although they're reactions, while fear is an emotion. Shocking, isn't it?

Scared Silly!

Sudden jolts of fear are useful in getting criminals to confess to their crimes. At least, that's what inventor H. A. Shelby must have thought when she patented a device in 1930 called "Apparatus for Obtaining Criminal Confessions and Photographically Recording Them." Here's how it's supposed to work: a criminal suspect is marched into a dark chamber; behind a partition is a person with a camera set up, waiting to capture the suspect's confession on film. And now for the fun part: mounted on the partition is a skeleton. At the right moment, the skeleton is lit up, scaring the willies out of the suspect. If he/she is criminal, a confession is sure to follow, and it's all recorded by the camera behind the skeleton. Whether or not it works, it's a nifty invention—no bones about it.

Snake Shock

Let's say I was to tell you that a loud noise would go "BANG!" right behind your head five seconds from now. Would you still flinch at the sudden noise? In a word, yes. That's your startle reaction working for you. Even one of the world's most famous scientists, Charles Darwin, couldn't suppress his startle reaction. He decided to test it by visiting a zoo and heading over to the glass terrarium where a venomous puff adder lived. Darwin's rational mind knew that a plate of glass was protecting him from the deadly reptile. He was determined not to jump back if the snake struck out at him. But the snake did strike, and Darwin leapt back very quickly. His conclusion: will and reason are nothing when matched with one's own imagination of a yet-to-be-experienced danger.

All About Your Amygdala

Why does a "BOO!" scare you? It's all in your head. Let's say you could flip open your skull and probe around in your spongy, slimy brain. You'd come across an almond-shaped bit—your amygdala (you've got two). One of the amygdala's jobs is to connect your emotions to your memories. Say you've been afraid of spiders since one walked across your leg. When you see a spider again, the amygdala connects back to that stored memory. Upon seeing something "scary," your amygdala sends a signal to your body to be ready to react to danger. It does this in a few thousandths of a second—i.e. fast! Then things get interesting. Turn the page to find out more. Prize for the reader who can turn the page in a few thousandths of a second…!

BOO!

Scary Monster

I bet I can make you readers cringe in fear with my terrifying knowledge!

Scary Monster, it's a little hard to be terrifying at an eighth-of-a-page tall. I'm sure the readers are far more awestruck by the larger, more frightening picture looming above me. Now if any readers get a papercut from turning this page, then at this size, I feast….

Bloodthirsty Vampire

Fright = Flight or Fight (with All Your Might)

STILL SCARED? IS YOUR HEART POUNDING? ARE YOUR PALMS NICE AND SWEATY AND MAKING A MESS OF THESE PAGES? GOOD! NOW IT'S TIME TO READ ON AND LEARN ABOUT WHAT'S GOING ON *ON* AND *UNDERNEATH* YOUR SKIN WHEN YOU'RE FULL OF FEAR.

Kidneys

Your adrenal glands are located on your kidneys. When they get the message from your amygdala (see Brain), the adrenal glands release the chemicals adrenaline and noradrenaline into your bloodstream. These make you super-alert and get your body prepared to meet the oncoming menace.

Sweat

You'll do a lot of this when you're scared. Sweat keeps your skin nice and slippery so enemies may have a hard time latching on to you. As your sweat evaporates, it will keep your body cool.

Taking It In

Do things around you seem strange? Does everything appear to be moving in slow motion? That's because when you're freaking out, your senses are heightened. Oh...if you're reading this book while traveling through a time warp, that might also explain it.

Your Socks

Smell awful. Really. You ought to change them some time.

Muscles

Your muscles tense so you're frozen into place. Your tense muscles are ready for you to run (the flight response) or stay and face the danger (the fight response).

Bladder and Colon

The bladder and colon produce and store your urine (pee) and feces (poo). In times of trouble, they get ready to get rid of whatever's inside to prepare you for violent action or injury.

Hair

The hairs all over your body stand up on end. Back when we were hairy cave-folk, all that raised hair would have made us look bigger and scarier.

Brain

Remember your amygdala (see page 7)? It helps you recognize dangers by sending an alarm message, with help from another part of the brain—the hypothalamus—to all the parts of your body that react to a scary experience.

Eyes

The pupils of your eyes dilate (get bigger) to let more light in. This helps you to see the danger better...even if you don't want to.

Saliva/Spit

You'll make less of this as your digestive system slows down.

Heart

Thump-thump-thump. Your heart beats like a kettle drum, pumping the blood faster and faster. This way it can get the blood to much-needed body parts, like your brain and muscles.

Lungs

The air passages in your lungs expand, allowing you to take in more air. The oxygen from the air will help your muscles flex, and move you where you need to be moved.

Stomach

The activity in your stomach slows to a standstill. Now that you're terrified, you don't have time to digest your food. Seriously. Stop eating!

Skin

You go pale—because the blood vessels constrict as the blood is diverted away from the skin and to the heart and your skeletal muscles (to get you pumped for some physical exertion).

Liver

Starts to break down glycogen, an energy-storing chemical, into a raw sugar called glucose to give you an energy boost.

Animal ArrrGH!

YOU'VE READ ABOUT WHAT YOUR BODY DOES WHEN YOU GET SCARED. MAYBE YOU DON'T LIKE ALL OF YOUR DEFENSIVE TACTICS AND WOULD LIKE TO TRY TO EMULATE SOME OF THE OTHER ANIMALS IN THIS GREAT WIDE WORLD. NATURE HAS A NUMBER OF WAYS POTENTIAL PREY ELUDES PREDATORS. WHY NOT TRY THESE THE NEXT TIME YOU GET SCARED?

Become Invisible

Okay, you're right, no animal is completely invisible. But there are a few animals that come equipped with a semi-transparent skin that allows light to pass through. Glance at a glass catfish, for instance, and you can see right to its stomach. However, even if the animal's internal organs are on display for all to see, they're usually colored to reflect the light streaming into the water from above, so are hard for a predator to spot. In the same way, a predator may stare right through the transparent wings of a glasswing butterfly and only see the leaf it's resting on.

Are You a Good Mimic?

Have you ever tried imitating every word of your parents, siblings, or teachers? They probably got annoyed very quickly. Some harmless animals have taken this concept to the max and developed to look or behave like other animals that can cause harm or injury. Scientists call this kind of disguise Batesian mimicry. For instance, to keep from getting eaten, some small spiders will mingle with ants they resemble. They'll even scuttle about on six legs and hold their remaining two front legs in the air to imitate the ants' antennae.

Roll Up into a Ball

When danger rears its head, some animals tuck theirs in and curl up into a ball. The pillbug and millipede are two invertebrates that do this; the pangolin (a scaly anteater) and the armadillo are two mammals that try this trick. What's working for all of these creatures is the bony armor that covers their backsides. Humans aren't quite so flexible, and can't roll up into the near-perfect spheres that some millipedes can. Even if we did, we don't have natural body armor to protect us. Instead, we'd leave our all-important spines out in the open to be chomped on. Try again!

Scary Monster

Bloodthirsty Vampire, did you know that many lizards, and animals like starfish, practice autotomy? That means losing a body part to save the whole animal. If a lizard is being attacked by a predator, for instance, it can drop its tail. The tail will keep twitching to distract the predator. The lizard suffers very little blood loss or serious injury, and will grow back its tail in time.

Hmmm. Too bad there's not more blood.

Bloodthirsty Vampire

Fright with Might

Some animals appear to "play dead" when in danger, perhaps so they won't seem as attractive to their predator— or maybe they just get so stressed out that they black out. Both the opossum and the eastern hog-nosed snake use this tactic, but only as a last resort. First, these animals will try: freezing and staying camouflaged; trying to appear bigger and more frightening (by rearing up and hissing); or running (or slithering) away.

Super-Duper Superstitions

Do you avoid walking under ladders? Do you sweat at the sight of a black cat? Are you always on the lookout for that perfect four-leaf clover? These kinds of superstitious actions are often motivated by fear—fear of what could happen if certain behaviors or rituals aren't performed, or fear that certain signals and events can bring misfortune.

12 + 1 = Superstition

Some people believe that the number 13 brings bad luck. Superstitious hotels or hospitals will avoid having a thirteenth floor, jumping from floor 12 to floor 14, or calling the thirteenth floor 12a or 12b. Thankfully, there are measures you can take to avoid coming into contact with this number. For example, if you're living in Paris and going to a dinner party with twelve guests, you can hire a *quatorzieme*, a professional fourteenth guest, to ensure that you'll be eating good food with good luck.

Mirror, Mirror, *Off* the Wall

Smash! A fallen mirror is never a good thing. Some people believe that breaking a mirror brings seven years of bad luck. The reason may stem from early beliefs that a person's reflection is part of his soul, so smashing the mirror can damage the soul. There are said to be ways to undo the bad luck, such as collecting the pieces of the mirror and throwing them in a river to wash away the ill fortune. That said, picking up sharp shards of glass with your bare fingers might bring bad luck of its own that can only be undone (or done up) with stitches. Be warned!

Knock on Book

Have you heard the expression "knock on wood"? People sometimes say (and do) this to ward off bad luck after commenting on their good fortune, which they hope will continue. Knocking on wood supposedly keeps bad luck at bay. This may come from an ancient belief that knocking a tree could keep evil spirits away, or perhaps summon helpful spirits. No matter. As we all know, books—like the one you're reading right now—are made from the pulp of trees. Do you feel a little nervous? Is bad luck heading your way? All you have to do is knock on book.

Yes, it's TRUE!
This book is made from
100% Real Wood!

Fear This Play

William Shakespeare, one of the best-loved playwrights of all time, is also known for penning a play that freaks actors out: *Macbeth*. On the night of the play's first performance, in 1606, one of the lead actors apparently died backstage. And because theater companies sometimes put on the play when they're running out of money—since *Macbeth* is popular with audiences—actors associate it with tough times. Some actors, fearing the play is unlucky, won't mention it by name, instead calling it *That Play* or *The Unmentionable*. If a superstitious actor says the play's name, a ritual can be performed to avoid the curse. The actor must leave the room, spin around three times, spit, then knock on the door and beg to be let back in.

Aggghh! Look at what page we're on! The author must be mad to have put us here!

Bloodthirsty Vampire, do you suffer from triskaidekaphobia—an irrational fear of the number 13?

Oh, that. No, no. No phobia. My fear is very rational. I just know the number 13 is pure evil, that's all.

NAMES FOR *MACBETH* MADE UP BY FEARFUL ACTORS	NAMES FOR *MACBETH* *NOT* MADE UP BY FEARFUL ACTORS
That Play	
The Scottish Play	
The Unmentionable	*Macbarf*
The Caledonian Tragedy	*Old Macdonald*
The Comedy of Glamis	*The Macarena*
	Macaroni and Cheese
	The New York Times

Curses! I Hope this Page Isn't Jinxed...

Have you ever had such a bad day that you thought you might be cursed? To believe in a curse means you think it's possible that a great power is causing you misfortune. For example, what if the text of thispagewasnot FORMATTED CORRECTLY? You know, like it was written in DIFFERENT FONTS and colors, and LOOKED LIKE A BIG OLD *mess*. Could this page be cursed? Read on and decide whether or not these other curses are true.

Curses Are for Babies

The "curse of the Bambino" was a way to explain why the Boston Red Sox weren't able to win the World Series for so many years. Bambino was a nickname for baseball great Babe Ruth, who helped the Red Sox win three World Series, the last in 1918. In 1920, the owner of the team needed money, and Babe Ruth was sold to the New York Yankees. At the time, the Yankees hadn't won the World Series. After acquiring Ruth, they won four World Series, and over twenty since. After selling Ruth to the Yankees, the Red Sox went 86 years without winning the World Series, which led many Boston fans to believe that the team was cursed. The "curse" lived on until 2004, when the Red Sox finally won the World Series.

When Nine Ain't Fine

Just in case you plan on becoming a famous composer, you might want to think twice about writing nine symphonies…if you want to avoid the "curse of the nines." Several famous composers, like Beethoven, Bruckner, and Schubert, died shortly after writing—or while writing—their ninth symphonies. One composer, Gustav Mahler, decided to give his *Ninth Symphony* another name (*The Song of the Earth*) and went straight on to his tenth, which, after believing that he'd avoided his fate, he called the *Ninth Symphony*. As it turns out, the symphony Mahler called the *Ninth* was the last he finished before he died. Apparently, nobody informed Mozart about the curse—he composed over forty symphonies!

Hope for Curses

One of the world's most famous gems, the Hope diamond, came from India, and was sold to a French traveler, Jean-Baptiste Tavernier, in the 1660s. The diamond has been owned by many of the rich and famous, including the kings Louis of France, from Louis XIV through to XVI. Tales of a curse surfaced in 1908, in newspaper stories that told how many of the diamond's owners had met untimely ends. According to legend, the diamond was really the eye of an idol that Tavernier had stolen. This theft placed a curse on the diamond's owner. But this "curse" smells like a hoax. One story said that Tavernier himself was torn apart by a pack of dogs. In reality, he lived to a ripe old age selling…what else?…diamonds.

Make Way for Mummy

People often put the words "curse" and "mummy" together. Why? In 1922, British explorer Howard Carter and his financier, Lord Carnarvon, discovered the tomb of the ancient Egyptian king Tutankhamen. King Tut, as he's often known, had died 3,300 years earlier, and was buried surrounded by his treasures. Five months after the discovery, Carnarvon died from blood poisoning attributed to a mosquito bite. The moment he died, all the lights in Cairo, Egypt, went out, and back in England, his dog fell dead at the same moment. The newspapers cried "Curse!" One reporter even made up a story of a curse written at the tomb's entrance. Later, people from museums in New York and Paris died after the museums exhibited some of Tut's treasures. But in 2002, a scientist in Australia conducted a survey of most of the people involved in the discovery of Tut's tomb. None of them had suffered an early death. In fact, the only one who had was Tutankhamen himself, who'd expired at around 18 years of age.

Fear of the Dark
Is No Walk in the Park

BEFORE YOU READ ANY FURTHER, *STOP*, WAIT UNTIL THE SUN SETS AND THE SHADOWS CREEP. (I MEAN IT. PUT THE BOOK DOWN.) NOW TRY READING THESE PAGES ALONE IN YOUR BEDROOM WITH JUST A FLASHLIGHT. SCARED OF THE DARK? YOU'RE NOT ALONE, BUT AS THESE PAGES WILL EXPLAIN, THERE'S A GOOD REASON WHY....

Why Fear Dark?

Darkness has the power to make you feel alone, simply because it cuts down on how much you can see around you. Even a familiar and safe environment, like your bedroom, can look strange and unfamiliar in the dark. Without light to reveal shapes properly, your imagination can fill in the gaps and make you think that the harmless pile of laundry sitting in the hallway is actually some giant blobby monster. The darkness brought on by night also brings out many creatures that could be living in your house, like silverfish and carpet beetles that munch on dust and carpets, or cockroaches emerging from the cracks in the walls to nibble at crumbs.

100% Pure Dark

Afraid of the dark? Well, fear no longer! This sample of 100% **Pure Dark** will help you conquer your fear. RESULTS GUARANTEED*. Simply stare at the sample shortly before confronting total darkness. Start building up your immunity to fear of the dark today!

Pure Dark sample is
YOUR FREE GIFT
for purchasing this book.

*Fine Print: Guaranteed Results apply only to overcoming a fear of the dark with a surface area of 2 inches x 2 inches. You have to overcome your fear of total darkness by yourself.

Like the Night

Nocturnal animals, which are active at night, are fans of the dark. Most do need *some* light to see, but their eyes are often larger in proportion to their faces than humans' are. And their pupils usually open more in low light to help them see better. The eyes of many nocturnal animals have a thin, skinlike layer of collagen (what your scars are made of) called the tapetum lucidum, which reflects light back into the eye. Leftover reflected light escapes back through the pupil. That's why if you see a cats' eyes in the dark, they glow when they catch light.

Dealing with the Dark

In the 1970s, scientists conducted an experiment using kindergarten–aged kids who were afraid of the dark. The kids were asked to say different things when left alone in a dark room. One group said, "I am a brave boy (or girl). I can take care of myself in the dark." The second group said, "The dark is a fun place to be. There are many good things in the dark." The kids in the first group did better than those in the second. Perhaps telling yourself you can deal with the dark is a more helpful way of thinking.

Night Fright

Today we live in an electric age with streetlights, patio lights, and night lights (not to mention corner stores that stay open twenty-four hours a day, seven days a week). To get rid of the dark, even at night, all we need do is flip a switch. But try flipping back in time to the Middle Ages (approximately 500–1500 CE). At this point in history, when night plunged the countryside into darkness, it stayed dark. More accidents were reported taking place in the night, like falling down stairs, into ditches, into toilets...you name it. Candles used for light were a big fire hazard. Some governments even spread fear of the night by establishing curfews to shut the city down. For instance, in the late 1300s in Sorbonne, France, the curfew bell rang at 9 pm. If you were caught out at night, you'd be fined the equivalent price of sixty loaves of bread. Staying out after your bedtime was enough to turn you into an honest-to-goodness criminal.

What's Scarier?

The power going out late at night or the power going out during the World Series?

Never Tire of a

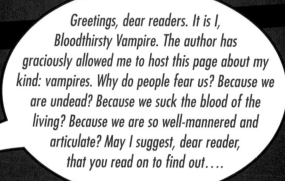

> Greetings, dear readers. It is I, Bloodthirsty Vampire. The author has graciously allowed me to host this page about my kind: vampires. Why do people fear us? Because we are undead? Because we suck the blood of the living? Because we are so well-mannered and articulate? May I suggest, dear reader, that you read on to find out....

Count on the Count

When you think of bloodthirsty vampires, one name always springs to mind: Dracula, the infamous count from Bram Stoker's famous novel. Stoker's book, published in 1897, popularized the idea that a vampire had no reflection in a mirror. Although Dracula is a fictional character, Stoker borrowed the name from a real prince named Vlad Dracula. He lived in Wallachia (near Transylvania) during the fifteenth century and tried to get rid of invading Turkish armies. Vlad Dracula, nicknamed "Vlad the Impaler," had a habit of impaling his victims on wooden stakes. It's only fitting that one of the ways the vampiric Dracula can be killed is by a wooden stake through the heart.

WHAT PHOBIA WOULD DRACULA *NOT* HAVE?

A. photophobia **B.** hemophobia **C.** catoptrophobia

Did you guess B? Right on! Hemophobia is a fear of blood. Considering a vampire's diet, Drac's unlikely to cower with fear at the sight of this red fluid. But photophobia (a fear of the light) and catoptrophobia (a fear of mirrors) are another story.

The Countess Is What Counts

Vicious Vlad wasn't the only real-life figure associated with vampirism. Flash back to the seventeenth century and over to Hungary to meet Elizabeth Bathory, a wealthy countess. If the legend is true (we don't know for certain), her last name could be eerily fitting. It's rumored she believed that drinking and bathing in human blood would keep her young. Too bad nobody from the future could time travel and give her some moisturizer. Instead, Bathory is said to have had her servant girls killed so she could take a dip in the tub. It all came to an end when Elizabeth was bricked up and trapped in her own room for the rest of her days.

Blood Sucking...Now with Tentacles!

Vampire legends aren't just about European nobility. Take the yara-ma-yha-who, from Australian Aboriginal folklore. This vampiric creature has a small body, a big belly, and a huge head with glowing eyes and jumbo jaws. It lives in fig trees and snatches its victims using octopus-like tentacles on its hands and feet. With its tentacles, the yara-ma-yha-who drains the victim of blood, but not enough to kill. The weakened victim is then swallowed whole, after which the yara-ma-yha-who drinks some water and naps. After that, it is said to regurgitate its meal—and the victim, surprisingly, walks away in one piece.

Greetings from Down Under!

Does misteltoe make you think of the custom of snatching a kiss under the plant during the holiday season? For a tree, mistletoe doesn't have such good associations. That's because mistletoe is a parasitic plant. Like leeches, ticks, and lice, a mistletoe clings onto another organism (in this case a tree) and feeds from it. A mistletoe plant has a bell-shaped structure at the tip of its root called a haustorium. As a young mistletoe grows, the haustorium penetrates the bark of the host tree to feed on its water and nutrients—sort of like how a vampire sucks blood from a warm human neck.

Spine-Tingling Sleep

WE SPEND OVER A QUARTER OF OUR LIVES ASLEEP. DOES THAT MEAN WE'RE PEACEFULLY RESTING OUR HEADS ON OUR PILLOWS WITHOUT A CARE IN THE WORLD? NO SUCH LUCK. MANY OF US—ESPECIALLY KIDS—HAVE AT LEAST ONE NIGHTMARE A WEEK. NO ONE REALLY KNOWS WHY WE HAVE NIGHTMARES AND WHAT THEY MEAN, BUT HERE ARE SOME FACTS TO KEEP YOU UP AT NIGHT....

Created by Fear

If you're lucky, your nightmares might get your creative juices flowing. That's just what happened to author Robert Louis Stevenson. Stevenson had a nightmare about a doctor who drank a weird powdered drink that turned him into a horrible, violent man. Three days later, Stevenson had written the first draft of his famous story *The Strange Case of Dr. Jekyll and Mr. Hyde*, published in 1886. According to Mary Shelley, her story of *Frankenstein* also came to her at night. She had a sort of waking vision of a corpse that was brought back to life by powerful machinery and was staring at a scientist with "yellow, watery, but speculative eyes."

Nightmares vs. Night Terrors

When you fall asleep, your brain activity goes through different stages. In certain stages, your eyeballs move around in their sockets, often producing rapid eye movements (known as REM). A **nightmare** is a long and frightening dream lasting from around five minutes to a half-hour that wakes you out of deep REM sleep, usually in the second half of the night. Often, nightmares are about something that can harm you (like falling off a cliff or a monster under your bed). They can happen several times in one night, and the nightmare itself can be repeated. A **night terror**, on the other hand, is a more intense reaction that wakes you up from sleep. It generally occurs earlier in the night before the deep sleep stage, and it's usually young kids (aged three to ten) who get them. Before waking up, someone with a night terror might thrash around in bed, sweat, or scream loudly. Luckily, once awake, the sufferer will likely forget what frightened her. Not so with a nightmare, which is often vividly remembered by the dreamer.

Bloodthirsty Vampire

Don't forget the horrifying nightmare of Elias Howe, an inventor from the 1800s. He dreamed that a group of fierce attackers was going to kill him. Howe noticed eye-shaped holes in their spears, which was the inspiration for the holes in needles for sewing machines, without which I would never be able to mend my capes!

No Horsing Around

Is the "mare" of a nightmare some crazy horse? Nope. The term "mare" could come from "mara," a female monster from Scandinavian folklore. According to legend, the mara sits on her victims' chests, causing suffocation. It's not far removed from tales of the old night hag, who also crushes the chests of sleeping people. The term "nightmare" could originally have been used to describe sleep paralysis.

ZZZZZZZZ...

These Pages Are Haunted!

Many ghost stories have turned out to be hoaxes, but other eerie occurrences have perplexed even scientists. Whether they rattle chains, turn up in recordings, or make a spooky appearance, hauntings by ghosts have been documented for thousands of years.

YIPE!

CLANG!

CLANG!

Things That Go Bump: Debunked

Poltergeists are mischievous ghosts who get blamed for unexplained sounds and movements. But there are explanations for some of the creaking and bumping "ghosts" might make in a "haunted" house. The doorway of an old house might be made from brick, steel, and wood. With changing temperatures, these materials contract and expand at different rates, making creaky or vibrating sounds when they rub together. Air that gets stuck in old plumbing may make weird noises as water moves through the pipes. And wind blowing against the soffit, the exposed underside of a roof, can cause a rattling.

First Ghost

The first ghost story written down took place around 40 BCE. Here's how it goes: a Greek philosopher named Athenodorus was short of cash and rented a house for a good price. Why was it going so cheap? The house was supposedly haunted. Athenodorus moved in, and sure enough, he soon heard rattling chains and saw a creepy old man walking into the garden. The old man pointed at a spot in the ground before suddenly vanishing into thin air. The next day, workers dug up an old skeleton and some chains nearby. Only when the bones were given a proper burial did the haunting stop. And, no, we don't know whether or not the rent went up once the ghost left.

Spook Sound

In 2003, a group of British scientists suggested that the creepy feeling people get in "haunted" houses might not be from ghosts after all. Instead, what's affecting them is a low frequency sound called "infrasound." The heavy bass sound of infrasound is so low that it's really hard to hear. It can cause anxiety, sorrow, and even give people chills. The British scientists tested out infrasounds on people attending a concert. Almost a quarter of the audience reported that they experienced unusual feelings when the infrasound was used. Infrasounds do occur naturally in storms and some earthquakes—two events that just so happen to freak us humans out.

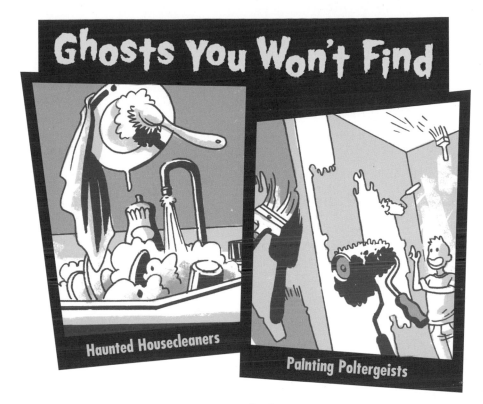

Ghosts You Won't Find

Haunted Housecleaners

Painting Poltergeists

A Host of Ghosts

Ghost experts have identified different types of spirits. The most common kind is the **crisis apparition**, which is the ghost of a living person (usually a close friend or relative) near the point of death. Crisis apparitions are described as solid and appear only once. **Replay ghosts** may appear when a person or animal dies violently. Just as their name suggests, they go through the motions of an event over and over again. **Cyclic ghosts** are like replay ghosts, only they appear on the same day once a year. Finally, there are **revenge ghosts**, which will haunt people with the intention of getting a message across or getting even with someone who may have wronged them in their lives. Others believe there's only one kind of ghost: the made-up kind. What do you think?

Scary Monster

Sounds that reach a low enough frequency can cause the eyeball to vibrate and make shapes appear in a person's peripheral vision—a possible explanation for ghosts themselves.

Ghosts Go Global

Say **CHEESE!**

The White House, Washington, DC

Many powerful figures have lived in this house, and some of them don't want to leave. One of the most famous phantoms of a former resident is Abraham Lincoln, who was assassinated in 1865. A famous, fake photo of Lincoln's wife reveals a ghostly image of Abe at her side. Lincoln's ghost apparently has been seen putting on his boots, and a story tells of his ghost knocking on the door of a visiting queen and scaring her...very unprofessional of an ex-president!

The World's Most Haunted Places

Has all this talk of ghosts got you thinking of packing your bags and heading to the nearest ghost-free destination? Think again! Sure, it's a big world out there, but every corner is haunted. Read up on some of the world's most haunted abodes.

Monte Cristo Homestead, Australia

The Crawley family was this famous home's first residents, in the 1880s. After her husband died, Mrs. Crawley only left the house twice in 23 years. Her spirit apparently still hangs around today. If it's ghosts you're after, this house takes the spectral jackpot: disembodied phantom faces have been spotted here; both friendly and unfriendly ghosts; a floating ghost; and a presence that kept people from walking up the stairs.

Christ Church Graveyard, Barbados

Usually it's pretty safe to expect coffins to stay still. That's what the Chase family in Barbados believed. However, in 1812, when their tomb was opened to add a family member, the heavy coffins inside were found scattered and overturned. They were rearranged and the tomb closed again. But over the years, each time the tomb was opened, the coffins were found rearranged. Finally, in 1820, the coffins were buried elsewhere in the cemetery. All has been quiet in the Chase tomb since.

Tower of London

Over the centuries, the Tower of London has been many things: a prison, a palace, a place of execution, and a museum. With all of the hangings, poisonings, beheadings, stabbings, and other deaths, as well as torture, that have taken place, it's no surprise that dozens of hauntings have been talked of here from as far back as the thirteenth century. One of the most famous of the tower's ghosts is Anne Boleyn, one of King Henry VIII's six wives, beheaded here in 1536.

Whaley House, San Diego

Known as the most haunted house in America, the Whaley House, built in 1857, was used as a theater, a billiard hall, and a courthouse. Some of the spooks reported to inhabit Whaley House are the original owner, a little girl, and a convict known as "Yankee Jim" Robinson, who was hanged on the property in 1852, five years before the house was built.

Borley Rectory, England

Whispers; a headless man; the ghost of a nun; sounds of a phantom coach; mysterious writing on the walls. These and other eerie events were said to have happened at the remote Borley rectory as far back as 1886. The people who moved there in the late 1920s were so spooked that they called a national newspaper. The paper brought the house to the attention of a famous ghost hunter, Harry Price. He hired forty researchers to document the goings-on in a year-long investigation. Though the rectory burned to the ground in 1939, it is still known as "the most haunted house in England."

Potential Holiday Spots?

Looking for a relaxing North American holiday spot? How about Terror Point (you can select either British Columbia or Nunavut for that destination)? Or there's always Terror Bay, Nunavut, or Terror Island in the Northwest Territories. And if those sound just too terrifying, there's always Cape Fear, North Carolina.

Science Goes Mad
(Aren't You Glad?)

When you think of a scientist, do you picture a wild-eyed man in a white coat working in a creepy, cluttered laboratory? The image of the "mad" scientist has been with us for many years. Here's how it got there....

Mad Science Is Old News

The mad scientist figure in movies, TV, and books is always tampering with dangerous new technology. But the beginnings of the mad scientist probably stretch back into our ancient past. Most cultures have stories about shamans and witch doctors. These are people with a great power that is often feared—also a trait of the mad scientist. Even *Frankenstein*, a story now almost 200 years old, has roots that stretch thousands of years back to ancient Greece and the myth of Prometheus. Prometheus was a creature called a Titan who stole fire from the all-powerful gods and brought it to earth. Dr. Frankenstein also stole a great power by creating a living creature from dead body parts.

Sparks in the Dark

If you watch a mad scientist movie, you'll likely see a lab with machines producing electrical sparks that climb between two vertical electrodes. These machines, Tesla coils, were invented by Nikola Tesla. Tesla, who invented the first practical alternating current motor in 1887 (which allows electricity to power everything from elevators to your computer's hard drive), was something of a "mad" scientist himself. He claimed he could split the earth like an apple, and said he could invent a death ray able to destroy 10,000 airplanes from 400 kilometres (250 miles) away.

To Be Perfectly Frank...

Mary Shelley's vivid nightmare became the tale of the famous mad scientist Dr. Frankenstein. In her story, a brilliant scientist gives a dead body new life. The creature is viewed as a murderous monster (after he's abandoned by Frankenstein), but the crazed creator is seen as just as monstrous. *Frankenstein* was published in 1818, during the Industrial Revolution, an era when factories began to appear. New machines made life easier for people, but some were fearful and saw *Frankenstein* as a warning tale about the dangers of new technology.

If you're watching a mad scientist movie on TV, thank Tesla. It's his famous coil that supplies the necessary voltage to power the picture tube.

Scary Monster

WHAT PHOBIA WOULD DR. FRANKENSTEIN *NOT* HAVE?

A. catagelophobia
B. atychIphobia
C. epistemophobia

Did you guess C? Right on! Epistemophobia is the fear of knowledge. The doctor would need knowledge to be able to learn how to reanimate dead tissue to create his infamous monster. But Frankenstein could suffer from catagelophobia, the fear of being ridiculed. And also atychiphobia, a fear of failure.

Experiments in Fear

NOW WE'RE GETTING INTO IT—THE SCIENCE OF FEAR. SCIENTIFIC EXPERIMENTS HAVE HELPED US SHOW WHAT FEAR LOOKS LIKE AND SMELLS LIKE. NO, LICKING THIS BOOK WILL NOT SHOW YOU WHAT FEAR TASTES LIKE. BETTER PUT THAT THOUGHT ASIDE AND READ ON....

Edging Along

In the 1950s, psychologist Eleanor Gibson was at the Grand Canyon when she noticed her baby crawling near the edge (don't worry—everything was fine). She and another researcher later decided to demonstrate that a baby would be aware of the danger of being at a cliff edge. The pair performed a famous experiment called the "visual cliff." It was a tabletop with a checkerboard pattern. Part way along, the table dropped down to make a pit at least one foot deep. The table was covered with a panel of strong glass so no one would actually fall down, but it created the illusion of a steep drop. The scientists let 36 babies crawl along their visual cliff (with their parents standing by). Only three crossed the glass, and those only did it because their parents were egging them on. Speaking of eggs, baby chicks when tested also stayed away from the deep end, as did baby goats and lambs.

Sniffing Fear

Does fear smell? Two U.S. researchers decided sniffing armpits was the way to find out. In their study, volunteers wore sweat-absorbing pads in their armpits while they watched a funny movie clip one day and a scary clip another day. After, their sweaty pads were removed and put into jars. A week later, the scientists asked people which pads smelled like happy people, and which smelled of terrified people. Many sniffers couldn't smell anything, but the ones who did picked out the fearful smell from men and the happy smell from men and women.

Watching a horror movie or sniffing armpit sweat pads?

Spreading Fear

In the animal kingdom, if one member of a flock or herd suddenly bolts at a sign of danger, the others follow suit. For a long time, scientists thought humans revealed their fear through language and facial expressions. But one study indicates that, as with other animals, our body posture and gestures are just as important in communicating fear. To test this, subjects of the study were hooked up to a machine that measured brain activity while researchers showed them photos of people, in different situations, with their faces blanked out.

Looking at the photos of people whose actions showed "fear" activated areas of the subjects' brains that would also respond to a fearful situation. This suggests that when a fearful moment strikes, we may not have time to look for the fearful contortions in another person's face, but a quick glance at the body may tell us all we need to know.

Who's Frightened?

As you now know, fear can be told from body language. So look at the two pictures. Which one of these two people is afraid? Look very, very carefully.

Face the Fear!

Though most often a human face is a comforting sight to us, at certain times the "look" or "stare" can also cause a scare. Spooky stares are known in every culture, and can be seen on masks, and even in nature. Take a look...if you dare (but don't stare)!

He Shoots, He Screams!

The masks and equipment worn by athletes in team sports not only protect players—they make them appear larger and more frightening. Think of a hockey goaltender. Let's say the goalie is scared to face the onslaught of the opposing team. The mask hides his or her expression. All that the other players can see is a big, skull-like mask before the net. Some goalies get "cage courage" with their masks on. By feeling more protected, they may play a tougher, more confident game. Case in point: Gerry Cheevers, who played NHL hockey in the 1960s and 70s. Cheevers was one of the first goalies to wear a mask with decorations. After a game in which Cheevers took a puck to the face, his trainer would paint a "scar" on his mask. Eventually, Cheevers' mask was littered with creepy stitch marks that also reminded spectators of just how dangerous a goalie's job is!

Scary Monster

There have been tiger attacks on humans in India and Malaysia. But people have tried wearing masks with big staring eyes on the *back* of their heads, and the number of tiger attacks apparently decreased. Maybe the tigers feel that they're being stared at, and think twice about making a surprise attack.

Keep an Eye Out

The eyes of someone surprised or afraid reveal more "white" than in any other human expression (happy eyes usually show the least amount of white). In an experiment, university researchers showed a group of volunteers pictures of faces with different expressions while they were in a brain scanner, each for only a fraction of a second—too fast for the volunteers to tell what they were looking at. The results of the experiment showed that the volunteers only reacted to the split-second images featuring the pictures of white-eyed terror. The conclusion: in a split-second, your brain will tell you you're seeing someone scared long before you can open your mouth to say "fear."

Face the Fear: 3 Easy Steps

Take this book and get to the closest mirror. OK, are you there? Now follow these instructions to make a fearful face:

1. Raise your upper eyelids as high as you can. You'll want to tense your lower eyelids—but keep your upper eyelids up.

2. Drop your jaw open. Then stretch your lips out wide and try to reach your ears with them.

3. Now raise your eyebrows as high as they can go. If you can, try to draw your eyebrows together while keeping them raised (if you can't—it's tough!—just keep them raised).

Go, Gorgon, Go!

Still don't think that stares can scare? Why not dip into Greek mythology and look at a Gorgon—just not right in the eyes. According to the myth, the most famous Gorgon, Medusa, had once been so beautiful that she enticed even a Greek god. One goddess was so jealous that she transformed Medusa into a creature with writhing snakes for hair, hands made from bronze, and eyes so fearsome that just one stare could turn any mortal being to stone.

Yes! The makers of *Fear This Book* have stumbled across the only **ACTUAL PHOTOGRAPH** of a Gorgon in existence. Several editors turned to stone trying to insert it into this book. One look, even from the photograph, will literally petrify. Do you dare to flip the page and stare at the Gorgon's face? Or are you too scared?

How do you feel when you hold this face for a while? One psychologist suggests that expressing fear—even a fearful look—makes you feel uncomfortable and scared. This happens across different cultures, since facial expressions tend to mean the same things around the world.

What's in the Water?

WHEN EARLY EXPLORERS FIRST STARTED TAKING TO THE OCEANS, THE SEA WAS A MYSTERIOUS REALM WITH DANGEROUS CURRENTS, FIERCE STORMS, AND HORRIBLE MONSTERS. WE KNOW MUCH MORE ABOUT THE DEPTHS OF THE OCEAN TODAY, BUT THAT DOESN'T MEAN THIS WATERY WORLD ISN'T WITHOUT A FRIGHT OR TWO.

Lake Leviathans

Who's the most famous deep water monster of them all? Scotland's Loch Ness Monster. Sightings of this giant lake (or "loch" in Scotland) monster reportedly date back at least 1,500 years. "Nessie" has a long narrow neck and small head, which have supposedly been snapped in a number of famous photographs—though most are too blurry to make out, and some have been admitted hoaxes. In 2003, the British Broadcasting Corporation bombarded Loch Ness with over 600 sonar beams, which only revealed an empty loch. But there may still be hope if you go looking for a lake monster. You could try searching Lake Okanagan in British Columbia for Ogopogo. Or there's the Lake Tianchi monster in China, and the Mokele Mbembe, said to inhabit Africa's Congo River.

Yoo-hoo! I'm ready for my close-up!

32

Triangle of Terror

On a map, trace a line with your finger from Bermuda to Puerto Rico to Miami, then back to Bermuda. That's the area known and feared as the Bermuda Triangle. The area has generated a lot of attention because of supposedly supernatural disappearances of airplanes and boats that have entered the triangle. The most famous disappearance took place in 1945, when a squadron of five U.S. military airplanes entered the triangle and vanished without a trace. Numerous exotic theories try to explain the "mystery." The triangle is one of two areas on earth where a compass needle points to the planet's true north pole (instead of its magnetic north pole), which could cause navigators to lose their bearings. Another explanation: the pilots were being led by a man who was not used to flying in the training grounds off the east coast of Florida. Yet another theory is that gas bubbles (methane hydrates) rise to the surface of the water, causing ships to sink.

Ape-Aged Anxiety?

Fear of the water that some of us have could stretch way back. Since monkeys and apes—our closest relatives—aren't the best swimmers, those that feared going near the water might have been the ones who went on to spread their genes to the next generation, and so on, until this fear became a part of who we *Homo sapiens* are.

See the Coelacanth

If it's ancient water creatures you're after, keep an eye out for a coelacanth. For years, scientists thought this 1.5 metre (5 foot) long fish was extinct, until fishermen in the Indian Ocean caught one in 1938. The fish looks the same as it did 340 million years ago, long before many famous dinosaurs were around.

Bloodthirsty Vampire

Bermuda Triangle? Baloney. I know an even scarier place.

Oh really?

Oh, yeah. Take your finger and trace a line from Auckland, New Zealand, to Brisbane, Australia, then on to Port Moresby, Papua New Guinea, to Suva, Fiji, and finally back to Auckland.

What on earth is that?

It's the South Pacific Quadrilateral! Told you it was terrifying!

Scary Monster

Oh, no! Someone has foolishly placed an orange box over the photo of the Gorgon! Now nobody will turn to stone. Drats!

Snapshot of Gorgon at the hair salon

Snakes:
Scares Start with "S"

BUNNY RABBITS. KITTENS. HAMSTERS. THESE ARE NOT ANIMALS THAT STIR UP FEELINGS OF FEAR. BUT WHAT ABOUT S-S-SNAKES?

Snake Scare

If you don't like snakes, you may be programmed that way. Some scientists feel that as early mammals developed, they learned to pick out danger signals in nature. A fear of snakes would not be unreasonable for early humans, who had to search in the bushes for food without thick hiking boots to keep their feet safe. Though most snakes are harmless, there are some species whose bites inject poisonous venom that can kill. Scientific research suggests that mammals (like ourselves) have devel-oped the ability to focus on potential-ly threatening animals like snakes and respond by feeling afraid...even if the snakes aren't out to get us. In one experiment, university students were shown pictures of scary things like snakes and spiders, and also "unscary" things, like mushrooms and flowers. The students reacted to the pictures of spiders and snakes much more quickly than they did to the flowers or mushrooms. No word on how quickly they reacted with fear to the marks on their final exams.

When Snakes Get Aped

We're not the only species to get scared by snakes. In Africa, primates like chimpanzees can freak out about seeing snakes in the wild. They'll shriek and even hurl sticks at them. Snakes don't have it any easier if they encounter vervet monkeys, another African species of primate that has developed a special alarm call just for snakes. It's a good thing that snakes are deaf and don't have to put up with all of that screaming.

No one really knows for sure if fear of snakes has been built into our genes or if it's a reaction we have taught ourselves. Evidence points to evolution. Madagascan lemurs, relatives of monkeys, don't show any fear around poisonous snakes, which are not found on the island.

Scary Monster

Games Primates Should Never Play

Snakes & Ladders

Egad—sticks and stones! They'll break our bones.

Not to mention spoil our picnic.

Arachnid
Anxiety

A SET OF LARGE FANGS. A FACEFUL OF SIMPLE EYES. WEBS GALORE. SPIDERS MAY BE LOVED BY SOME, BUT MANY PEOPLE HAVE MORE FEAR THAN LOVE FOR THESE EIGHT-LEGGED ANIMALS.

Actual size of the goliath bird-eating tarantula.

Where Spiders Aren't Spooky

Although often feared in the western world, not everyone lives in fear of arachnids. In some parts of Africa, local people clean and protect spider homes. In fact, a West African myth features a spider hero named Anansi who is able to bring upon rain to stop raging fires. Spiders, common pets in some parts of Brazil, are also becoming popular in North America…though they're not man's best friend yet.

Actual size of the author's pen...

When Spiders Get Funky

During the Middle Ages in southern Europe, the harmless wolf spider was blamed for causing an illness known as tarantism, which makes people sweat, grow weak, and get the shakes (of course, so does sunstroke). It's been written that tarantism was treated not by a good night's rest, but by three to four days of solid dancing! And not just any dance, but a crazy "tarantula dance," also known as the tarantella. The dance, the illness, and the spider name "tarantula" all come from the village name, Taranto, Italy, where the sickness was blamed on the spiders. FYI: the tarantula is unrelated to the wolf spider that was blamed in the first place.

Eight Legs = Ewwwww!

We may fear them for the same reason we may fear snakes: because some spiders are poisonous, we've developed the ability to recognize them as a potential danger. But although almost all spiders' bites contain venom to subdue and kill their prey, the bites of most spiders won't harm humans because their fangs are too small to break our skin. Only 0.1 per cent of the 40,000 known spiders in the world have bites that could hurt or kill humans. (For people who don't like math, that equals only 40 kinds of spiders in the world capable of delivering a deadly bite.)

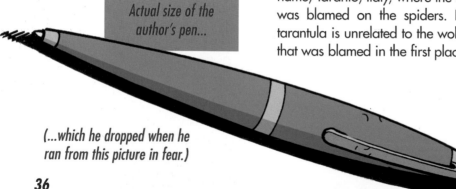

(...which he dropped when he ran from this picture in fear.)

With its legs spread wide, the goliath bird-eating tarantula is actually bigger than a page of this book. Like me, it's got big fangs, except this arachnid uses its fangs to inject venom into its victim. The venom, in combination with digestive juice vomited onto its victim from the stomach, turns it into a gooey soup that is sucked back up. That's my kind of animal!

Bloodthirsty Vampire

Maligned
and Misunderstood

IT ISN'T JUST SNAKES AND SPIDERS THAT SCARE US. THERE IS A WHOLE HOST OF ANIMALS THAT HUMANS HAVE GIVEN A BAD RAP. IN HORROR STORIES AND MOVIES THEY MAY OFTEN BE PORTRAYED AS MONSTERS, BUT IN REALITY, HUMAN EXPLOITATION OF THESE ANIMALS AND THEIR HABITATS IS THE REAL KILLER.

Hats off to Bats

Don't let bats bug you, since they're a huge help when it comes to bug control. Bugs are like potato chips to these winged mammals. Each night, a bat typically eats around half its body weight in insects. And contrary to popular belief, bats won't get tangled up in your hair. That's because most bats find their way by bouncing high-frequency sounds off objects around them—it's called echolocation. Echoes caused by the sounds bouncing back to the bats can help them locate obstacles or prey.

Bloodthirsty Vampire

Want to impress your family with your astounding vocabulary? Try these words on for size. **Microchiropterans** are the bats that use echolocation to find their food, usually insects. They're "micro" bats because they're usually much smaller than the **megachiropterans**. These bats are called "mega" since they're among the larger bats. They use their sense of smell to sniff out a meal, often fruit and nectar.

BAT BITS AND BITES

Number of Species: 1,100
Smallest Bat: bumblebee bat (around the size of a penny and the weight of a dime)
Largest Bat: flying fox (wingspan is 1.8 metres/6 feet—in other words, about the length of 8 copies of this book laid end-to-end)

Vampires Don't Suck

First of all, vampire bats don't suck: they lap blood with their tongues. And of the 1,100 species of bats in the world, only three drink blood. These small winged mammals come out at night while their favored prey is fast asleep: cows, horses, pigs, and big birds (humans are not typically on the diet). After biting their prey with razor-sharp teeth, vampire bats spit out chemicals that keep the blood flowing. Vampire bats don't drain large animals of their essential fluids. In a twenty minute sitting, they'll drink around 25 millilitres (2 tablespoons) of blood. If they can't drink for more than two nights in a row, they can starve. That's when these bats can become really giving. If a vampire bat with a full belly of blood comes across a starving bat from its own roost, it will regurgitate some of its meal to help out the hungry. A friend indeed!

Why Shriek at Sharks?

You'll recall from page five of this book that I used to be terrified of sharks. I'm not alone. Shark attacks are sensationalized, often making international headlines. In fact, only a few species of sharks have been known to attack humans; even fewer to eat them. Many shark attacks are a case of mistaken identity. Take the great white shark, the one that "starred" in the *Jaws* movies. Some of its favorite foods are sea lions and dolphins, which are about our size. From the water below, the silhouette of a surfboard or a swimmer can look pretty close to a tasty sea lion. Other times, the shark may be defending its feeding ground, thinking people are trying to use it. When a shark does attack, it usually takes a test "chomp" first. In many attacks on humans, a shark only bites once before realizing the bony body is not the meal it intended. To stress this once more: shark attacks are rare. In North America, you're more likely to get killed by a tornado or a bolt of lightning, or even from an alligator attack, than a shark.

Scary Monster

Do you know what's less than 1 metre (3 feet) long? More than half the world's sharks!

Yuck—*humans!* I'll stick to the sea lion sub.

Very good, sir.

Today's Special
Hot Humanburger
with Kelp Salad

SHARKS: ESSENTIAL INFORMATION

Number of Species: nearly 500
Number of Species Known to Attack Humans: 32
Average Number of Shark Attacks per Year: around 50, with fewer than 10 fatalities
Average Number of Sharks Killed by Fishers per Year: 30 to 100 million
Smallest Shark: dwarf lantern shark (17 to 20 centimetres/7 to 8 inches long)
Largest Shark: whale shark (15 metres/50 feet long); it eats mostly tiny plankton and small fish, straining them through a baleenlike filter in its mouth.

Discussing the
Disgusting

FEAR AND DISGUST ARE BOTH EMOTIONS THAT WORK TO PROTECT US. JUST AS WE FEAR A SITUATION THAT MIGHT CAUSE US IMMEDIATE DANGER, DISGUST IS MEANT TO KEEP US FROM HARM.

Roach Revulsion

Why does the cockroach instill that disgust reaction? Roaches themselves actually spend more time keeping clean than we do. They clean and groom themselves whenever they need to. How often do you hop in the shower because you've got a speck of dirt on you? The problem is that roaches don't see any difference between living in a garbage can or on your kitchen counter, and they can easily spread germs from one place to another. They'll also happily nibble on any food you leave out, and once they eat, they have no problem excreting all over your kitchen counter. Yummy.

What's Scarier?

Spending hours cleaning a cockroach-infested home or spending hours washing yourself?

It's a Gross Universe

Disgust literally means "bad taste," so it's no wonder that certain animals that can get into our food truly revolt us. Many insects, like flies and cockroaches, have a tendency to hang around human food. Since an animal like a blowfly doesn't wash its legs when it flies from a pile of poop to a hamburger on the grill, it could spread harmful bacteria from the poop. In other words, these animals may disgust us because, deep down, we fear they may make us sick. Perhaps the ancestors of humans who developed a disgust of these animals avoided getting sick, and lived on to spread this emotional response.

Survey of Yuck

In the late 1990s, a researcher from the London School of Hygiene and Tropical Medicine interviewed people from around the world on what they found disgusting. Bodily fluids, wounded body parts, rotting food, and animals like lice, maggots, and dogs and cats topped the list. What do they have in common? All of these things can spread disease. In a further study, over 40,000 people looked at pictures of objects on the Internet. It was found that people were disgusted by items connected with disease. For instance, people who looked at a picture of a towel soaked in a blue stain weren't grossed out, but pictures of a towel supposedly soaked in bodily fluids (a yellow/red stain that looked like blood and pus) revolted them.

Big Bug Love

Bugs and insects are frequently targeted as objects of horror, and have become movie stars because of it. In the 1950s, "terrifying" bug movies swarmed across movie theaters. The bigger the bug, the better. Giant ants menaced the desert in *Them!*, while a huge praying mantis attacked New York and Washington in *The Deadly Mantis*. Other giant arthropods also became movie menaces, from *Tarantula* to *The Black Scorpion*. Still, insects aren't just huge movie monsters, they're hugely important animals on the planet. Insects pollinate plants; they work as recyclers, breaking down decaying matter (who do you think eats the animal poop that collects around us?); and they're also a key link on the food chain. Take away insects, and many other animals would starve. We may fear insects from time to time, but never underestimate their importance.

Mondo Monsters

MONSTERS: HELPFUL OR HORRIFYING? GOING WAY BACK, PEOPLE HAVE USED MONSTERS TO REPRESENT UNKNOWN THINGS ABOUT THE WORLD, AND TO GIVE SHAPE TO OUR FEARS. IT'S HARD TO EXPLAIN WHY YOU'RE AFRAID OF YOUR DARK CLOSET TO SOMEBODY, BUT IF YOU SAY A SCARY MONSTER LIVES INSIDE OF IT, YOU'VE GOT A MUCH BETTER REASON TO KEEP IT CLOSED AT ALL TIMES.

Wowie zowie! My own page to talk about scary monsters. It's all I ever wanted...at least, aside from a more stylish set of bandages. Sit back and enjoy this menagerie of monsters, if you dare....

Bring on the Bogeyman!

He could be outside your bedroom window. Or lurking in the closet. Or even under your bed, waiting for you to put this book down and drift off to sleep. The bogeyman is a monster that kids have been told about for hundreds of years in a number of cultures, most often by parents who warn their young to stay away from dangerous situations or else the bogeyman will come. What exactly do we know about him? Very little, except that he is a figure to be feared. It's probably this unknown quality to the bogeyman that makes him so scary—that, and the fact that he often comes to "get you!"

Zombies Alive!

We've looked at ghosts, the spirits of the dead lacking bodies. Zombies are kind of the opposite: a body without a spirit to guide it. Many movies have been made about the dead coming back to life, walking a little more slowly than usual, and looking pretty blank-faced...until they rip you to pieces and eat your flesh! There was one apparent case involving a real-life zombie back in 1936. A dazed woman was found wandering about in Haiti. This may not sound out of the ordinary, but get this: the woman was recognized by her family, who claimed she'd died back in 1907, nearly 30 years earlier.

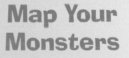
Scary Monster

Real-life zombies? That's *terrifying*!

If only it were true. A report from a doctor on the scene who cared for the woman says it was a case of mistaken identity. That leaves only one undead person on this page. Me.

You're a real-life zombie? That's *terrifying*!

No, no, no. I'm just a bloodthirsty vampire.

Phew. That's a load off my mind.

Bloodthirsty Vampire

Map Your Monsters

On early maps, monsters were sometimes marked onto still unknown areas, like parts of Asia and Africa, to suggest that explorers hadn't reached them yet. A map from the 1200s has a dragon placed in southern Africa. One 1400s map puts a dragon in Asia, with some text warning travelers of huge men with horns, and serpents that eat oxen whole. But what about the elephantlike creature with two long teeth, described on a 1516 map of Norway? Is it a dragon? A terrifying mutation? Nope. Just a walrus. Not one specific walrus, but an image of those exotic creatures that explorers had found there.

A Spring in His Step

Okay, so "Spring-Heeled Jack" is not the most terrifying name you've ever heard, but this bizarre man–creature sighted in England between 1837 and the early 1900s reads like Batman's creepy evil brother: large pointed ears, glowing red eyes, sharp claws, and a mouth that breathed flames. Oh, and he attacked people, too. Though few were seriously hurt, there's at least one story involving Jack breathing fire into someone's face (not nice, Jack). This living jack-in-the-box's major claim to fame were his superhuman leaps: in one bound he could jump from the ground to the roof of a house. Boing!

[More Monsters]

Werewolf? Here Wolf!

Imagine it's a dark night: you're on your way to your grandmother's in your hooded red outfit. The clouds pull away to reveal a full moon. Suddenly, a hairy man with big eyes, ears, and teeth stops to ask for directions. At this point, you're probably shouting "werewolf!" Actually, in this case, it's only a lost backpacker. Don't feel duped. The wolf has been used as a symbol of fear for thousands of years in myths, fairy tales, and still to this day, in horror movies. The stereotypical werewolf is a shape-shifting human who turns into a shaggy wolf by the light of the full moon. Sometimes, only silver bullets seem capable of stopping this creature.

Wolf Crimes

Werewolves star in movies today, but their history dates back to Norse mythology. Fierce warriors, called berserkers, wore the skins of animals and took on the savage qualities of bears and wolves. In battle they ignored pain, and killed as many as they could. An ancient Greek myth tells the story of a man, Lycaon, who was transformed into a wolf after dining on human flesh. In the mind of Greek god Zeus, he'd become nothing more than an animal. By the 1400 and 1500s, Europe was a werewolf playground. France had a bad wolf problem; packs of wolves were known to enter Paris and attack people. In 1603, a series of attacks by a wolf–creature were described. A culprit, Jean Grenier, confessed to the crimes—but blamed it on the fact that he had transformed into a werewolf at the time. The court passed judgment that Grenier was in fact a werewolf and locked him up in a monastery. That's a pretty light sentence when you consider that Stubbe Peeter of Germany was burned in 1590 for the same reason.

THINGS WEREWOLVES DO	THINGS WEREWOLVES DON'T DO
Howl at the moon	Shave
Dodge silver bullets	Buy nail clippers
Wear wool sweaters without a t-shirt underneath	Eat soufflé
Attend full moon parties	

Another French Beast

France's wolf–creature problems persisted even into the 1760s. Between 1764 and 1767, there were reports of a bizarre creature that carried out a series of attacks in the French province of Gévaudan, killing around 60 people. The monster was described as being "wolflike," had a tuft of hair (like a lion) at the end of its tail, and was around the size of a cow. Just what was this beast? Some say the animal was actually one or a group of crazed people; others assert it could have been an escaped lion.

A Devil of a Monster

The heavily forested Pine Barrens in the U.S. state of New Jersey was the supposed site of a weird, bipedal creature with a horse's head and hooves, and batlike wings. Known as the Jersey Devil, this unusual beast dates back to the 1700s. For a week in January 1909, it is said to have gone on a reign of terror. It left tracks all over Burlington, New Jersey, attacked a trolley car, and got sprayed with a hose by a local fire department. One thing it didn't do was play hockey—but it did inspire the name for New Jersey's NHL team.

Freaky Fairy Tales

PICTURE YOURSELF BEING TUCKED INTO BED AND BEING READ A FAIRY TALE BEFORE YOU FALL ASLEEP. NOW LET'S TAKE A CLOSER LOOK AT A FAIRY TALE AND ITS INGREDIENTS: MONSTERS, VIOLENCE, TERRIFYING FORESTS, WICKED STEPPARENTS. FAIRY TALES ARE A RECIPE FOR NIGHTMARES! WHY HAVE GROWN-UPS BEEN SCARING CHILDREN WITH THEM FOR HUNDREDS OF YEARS?

Get Grim with the Grimms

Once upon a time (actually, in the early nineteenth century), there were two German brothers, both law school graduates, who were trying to get their careers off the ground. A good friend was looking for a collection of folktales to publish. The brothers wandered the countryside and libraries collecting tales for their friend. These folktales hadn't been considered stories for children, but the brothers decided to publish the stories under the title *Children's and Household Tales*. You may know the brothers better as the Grimms. Their fairy tales include *Hansel and Gretel*, *Ashputtle* (a.k.a. *Cinderella*), and *Little Red Cap* (a.k.a. *Little Red Riding Hood*).

A wicked stepmother with a poisoned apple or a "wicked" stepmother with a list of chores?

WHAT PHOBIA WOULD CINDERELLA *NOT* HAVE?

A. novercaphobia
B. hyalophobia
C. poinephobia

Did you guess B, hyalophobia? That's the fear of glass. As Cinderella slipped her foot into a glass slipper in some versions of the story, let's assume that she didn't fear it. But Cinderella could have suffered from novercaphobia, a fear of one's stepmother. Similarly, she could have developed poinephobia, a fear of punishment.

Proceed with Caution

Although the details of fairy tales can be gory, getting a healthy scare from a fairy tale might make you reconsider dangerous situations in real life, such as a stranger inviting you into his home for treats (like that witch in *Hansel and Gretel*). By entering the world of the story, fairy tales give readers a way to experience their fears in a safe environment. What's it like to be abandoned by one's parents? Many fairy tales feature orphans, or parents who don't love their children. Do your older siblings torment you? Are they as bad as Cinderella's cruel step-sisters? A kid can't live at home forever, and will have to venture into the wide world and grow up. Many fairy tales feature characters that venture away from home.

Alternate Endings

Since they were stories told from one generation to another in different cultures and communities, fairy tales often have different details and endings. For instance, in the brothers Grimm version, Little Red Riding Hood is eaten alive and later saved by a hunter who cuts the wolf open to free her. However, a version written by Charles Perrault sees the wolf getting the chance to digest his meal without interruption from a hunter. This is followed by a verse warning kids not to be lured by strangers—but makes no mention of being lured by talking wolves....

Fairy-less Tales

Take a good look at many fairy tales and you'll often find a host of horrifying creatures: goblins, evil witches, devils, gnomes, giants; in fact, just about everything except fairies. The reason is probably because when these stories were translated into English from German, the English upper-classes thought they were written for children, and gave them the name "fairy tales" to enchant young audiences (and perhaps keep grown-ups away from them). However, most of the original fairy tales were written as cautionary fables for adults. Take a look at an old fairy tale that hasn't been edited and watered-down into an animated movie. These stories contain grisly details in which all sorts of gory things happen. For example, in *Ashputtle*, the two wicked step-sisters cut parts of their feet off so they'll fit into Ashputtle's slipper. At Ashputtle's wedding to the prince, the wicked stepsisters show up and get their eyes pecked out by birds. There's something you don't see in an animated family movie!

...and they lived miserably ever after. The End!

Favorite Fairy Tales

The Fairy Tale
Survival Guide

This handy dandy Fairy Tale Survival Guide offers indispensible advice on avoiding fairy tales'—and life's—pitfalls. Tip: don't play in deep, dark forests. And learn to trust your instincts. When someone invites you into her gingerbread house, think about it. Who in their right mind makes a house from gingerbread?

Dark Forest

Sooner or later, you may reach a moody-looking forest. It may look like a fun place, but beware! Wolves, wicked witches, ax-wielding woodsmen—you name it, they love to hang out here. The forest is vast and full of danger. Trees tower above kids, and the thick canopy of leaves blocks out the sunshine. In a fairy tale, anything could pop out of the bushes. Some people think the wild and untamed forest represents what it's like to grow up and "find yourself." By emerging from the forest, we become more developed and ready to become adults.

Troubled Home

Families in most fairy tales aren't happy. Sometimes the parents are dead, neglectful of the kids, the plumbing is terrible...you get the idea. This gives the fairy tale kids a reason to leave home and make their way on their own. If you find yourself in a fairy tale, doing a ridiculous amount of chores, put that broom down and get out.

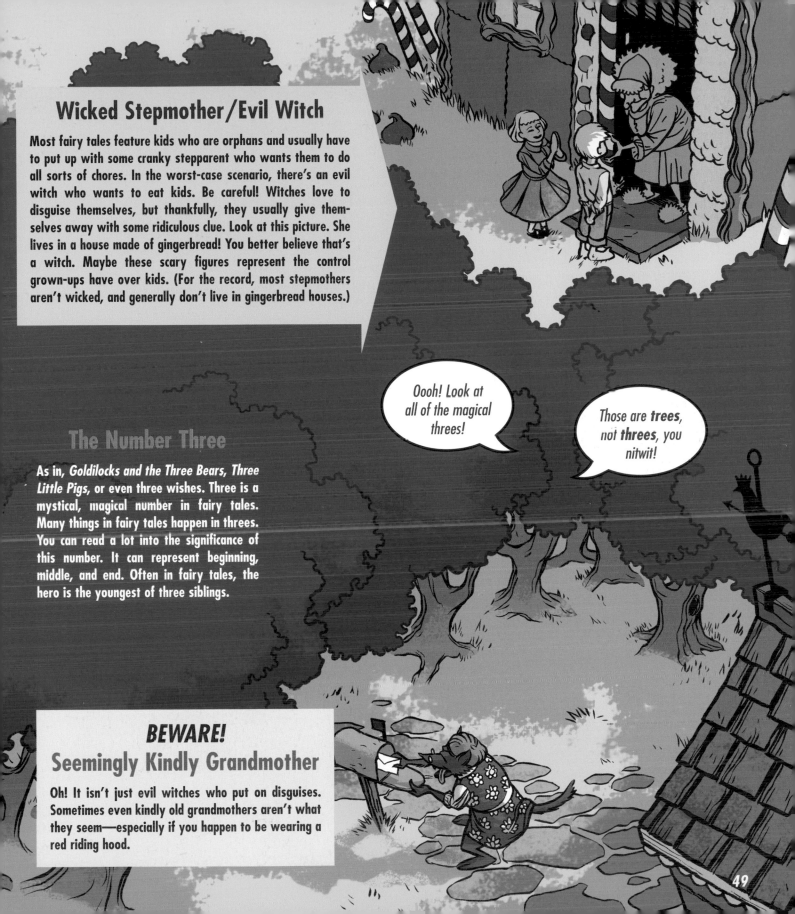

Wicked Stepmother/Evil Witch

Most fairy tales feature kids who are orphans and usually have to put up with some cranky stepparent who wants them to do all sorts of chores. In the worst-case scenario, there's an evil witch who wants to eat kids. Be careful! Witches love to disguise themselves, but thankfully, they usually give themselves away with some ridiculous clue. Look at this picture. She lives in a house made of gingerbread! You better believe that's a witch. Maybe these scary figures represent the control grown-ups have over kids. (For the record, most stepmothers aren't wicked, and generally don't live in gingerbread houses.)

The Number Three

As in, *Goldilocks and the Three Bears, Three Little Pigs,* or even three wishes. Three is a mystical, magical number in fairy tales. Many things in fairy tales happen in threes. You can read a lot into the significance of this number. It can represent beginning, middle, and end. Often in fairy tales, the hero is the youngest of three siblings.

Oooh! Look at all of the magical **threes**!

Those are **trees**, not **threes**, you nitwit!

BEWARE!
Seemingly Kindly Grandmother

Oh! It isn't just evil witches who put on disguises. Sometimes even kindly old grandmothers aren't what they seem—especially if you happen to be wearing a red riding hood.

BOO!

Go with the Phobia

YOU MIGHT FEEL THREATENED BY GLANCING AT A VENOMOUS BLACK WIDOW SPIDER. FAIR ENOUGH. BUT WHAT IF THE BLACK WIDOW WAS KEPT SAFELY BEHIND GLASS AT A ZOO? WOULD YOUR HEART STILL RACE WITH A FEELING OF PANIC THAT THE SPIDER MIGHT SOMEHOW GET TO YOU? IF YOUR FEELINGS OF INTENSE FEAR OUTWEIGH THE ACTUAL DANGER AND YOUR FEAR CAUSES SIGNIFICANT DISTRESS IN YOUR LIFE, YOU MIGHT JUST HAVE A PHOBIA.

Defining the Phobia...

A phobia is the fear of an object or a situation that is out of proportion to the actual threat. The fear is usually beyond voluntary control, and may cause the sufferer to avoid circumstances in which he might encounter that fear, often interfering with his quality of life. So, in this case, someone who is so afraid of spiders might keep away from a zoo altogether. This is known as a **situational phobia**. A **social phobia** is the overwhelming fear of appearing foolish in front of others—so much so that the phobic might avoid situations in which she feels others will judge her. **Agoraphobia** is the fear of being trapped in a position where you might panic out of the blue and lose control. Agoraphobics often avoid public places. It's estimated that around 5 to 12 per cent of North Americans suffer from phobias.

...And How To Get One

Research suggests there are three types of experiences that may lead to someone developing a phobia. A **traumatic event** (say, like falling into a crate full of wriggling spiders) could bring on a phobia. You might also acquire a phobia through **modeling**. No, not the kind where you dress up and walk down a fashion runway. Modeling means that by watching a parent or loved one get freaked out by spiders, for instance, you might then model their behavior and learn that spiders are scary. A phobia also may arise from **information transmission**. For instance, someone or something you trust (like your teacher or a newspaper) might say you should be afraid of spiders (or supermodels). You might not fear either spiders or supermodels, but you could start to fear them on the basis of the expert's opinion.

Is the author an expert of some kind?

I don't know. I think he went to university once. Why?

Well, the title says, "Fear This Book." So...should we?

Bloodthirsty Vampire

Scary Monster

PLACES TO PUT PHOBOS' IMAGE
Ancient Greek shields

Meet Phobos

The word phobia comes from the Greek word *phobos*, which means fright. It was also the name of an ancient Greek god who could strike terror into his enemies. Legendary hero Heracles had an image of the horror-god on his shield, possibly to scare his foes. Phobos is described as having eyes glowing with fire, and a mouth full of terrible but glittering white teeth. This can only mean one thing: Phobos probably saw his dentist at least twice a year, but should have considered visiting an ophthalmologist.

PLACES *NOT* TO PUT PHOBOS' IMAGE
Wallpaper for the baby's nursery

BIBLIOPHOBIA:
Instant Cure!

Do you suffer from *bibliophobia*? That means you have an irrational fear of books. Guess what? You're reading a book right now. Congratulations, you're cured!

Fear These Words!

If you like books like this one, you must like the words in them (and the pictures, too). So what about the word pneumonoultramicroscopicsilicovolcanoniosis? Or floccinaucinihilipilification? Or antidisestablishmentarianism? Are these words hard to pronounce? Do they appear as a string of incomprehensible letters? Do they make you perspire uncomfortably? Do you feel nervous and edgy? You may be afflicted with a condition known as **hippopotomonstrosesquippedaliophobia**. It's a real phobia, alright—the fear of long words!

[On with the Phobia]

Old Phobias: A Theory

It's been suggested by a psychologist that as humans evolved, we were left with the ability to develop phobias of the kinds of dangers our primitive ancestors would have feared—like snakes and spiders. That would explain why we don't have many pho-bias for the more deadly objects of our modern era. For instance, you're more likely to get injured by sticking your finger in an electrical socket than by dangling it in front of a garter snake—yet a fear of plugging in household appliances is rare indeed.

Don't Look Down!

It's natural to fear heights, but there's a difference between being concerned for your safety at a steep cliff edge and freaking out on an enclosed apartment balcony. A phobia of heights is known as **acrophobia**. With treatment called **exposure therapy**—which involves preparing for, then eventually actually traveling high up in a building to look over the balcony—it's often very curable. With exposure therapy, phobics can gradually expose themselves to their phobia to ensure that they're not overwhelmed by it. By looking over the balcony bit by bit you can control the fear, rather than it controlling you. If you stay out there long enough, you might even enjoy the view.

In a Tight Spot

Claustrophobia is the fear of cramped spaces. It may be related to an ancient fear of predators that trapped their prey in a small, confined area—the way that a team of lions will slowly encircle their prey before pouncing for the kill. From laboratory tests, it has been observed that a great number of claustrophobic panics involve a shortness of breath and a fear of suffocation. Around 2 per cent of the population has severe claustrophobia. If you suffer from this, you might feel so frightened of getting trapped in small rooms or elevators that you'll avoid them so you don't suffocate or freak out in front of other people. You may even choose to take the stairs—a healthier choice, but more challenging if you're headed to the fortieth floor.

High-Tech Phobia Fighting

Exposure therapy may not be new, but in today's high-tech world, some phobics can try out a modern way of facing their greatest fears. Virtual reality exposure allows phobics to experience a simulation of the situation or object they fear. Like something out of a science fiction film, virtual reality exposure requires that phobics put on a headset with earphones and small TV monitors inside, so they can see and hear a simulated experience. They have the illusion of going inside the computer-generated world to face their fear. This gives a phobic control over the situation without having to leave the therapist's office. There's an airplane simulation, complete with a chair set up to mimic the bumps of air turbulence. Other environments include a virtual elevator or a suspended bridge. And there's even a program that lets patients touch a toy spider while looking at an image of a spider.

NEVER COMING TO A THERAPIST'S OFFICE NEAR YOU...
Virtual reality exposure therapy for people who fear technology

I Don't Want to Go to School!

Have you ever faked sick or just felt stressed out about going to school? It's been estimated that 10 per cent of kids have a mild fear of school, and 1 per cent have a more serious fear. There are many reasons young kids might be afraid: fear of leaving home and parents, new teachers, bullying, or not doing well in school.

Keep 'Em Separated

School phobia is an anxiety about leaving home and going to school. It's based around one of our early fears: abandonment. Unlike reptiles, which are ready to roam in the wild shortly after birth, we need our parents' nurturing to get us through our early years. Without a caregiver, we might not survive. It's been observed that the heart rate of infants goes up when they're separated from their moms. For some kids, leaving the safety of home and the care of their parents could send them spinning a web of fear.

Testing, One-Two-Three...

Put this book down and take out a piece of lined paper. NOW! In the next five minutes, you are to summarize the first fifty pages of this book using complete sentences and proper grammar. How you perform on this test will determine what college you'll attend. Stressed? One of the biggest fears to be found in a school is test anxiety. There are a number of different reasons for it: feeling the weight of the expectations of your parents or teachers, or feeling a lack of control under pressure. The best advice is simple and you already know it: study and be prepared.

Bees' Knees ELEMENTARY SCHOOL

They're All Going to Laugh at You

Do you sweat at the thought of having to spend all day in a crowded classroom? Social phobia is the fear of being viewed negatively by other people in a social or group setting. The fear isn't that the people are going to attack you, but that everyone's watching your every move and that you'll look like a fool in front of them. It's natural to feel nervous in front of a crowd if you're delivering a speech to the class, but a persistent and strong fear of these kinds of social situations, even something as simple as sitting down for a bite of a sandwich in the lunch room, could indicate the presence of this common phobia.

Screee-atch!

Has some classroom joker—not you of course—ever scraped fingernails against the blackboard to cause that horrible noise that sets your hairs on end and a shiver down your spine? In the 1980s, a group of scientists decided to explore what about that sound makes us cringe. Twenty-four participants listened to some pleasant sounds, like running water or chimes, and some annoying sounds, like rubbing Styrofoam together and scraping the black-board. Blackboard-scraping was rated the most awful sound of all. It was observed that the annoying sound is close to the warning cry of macaque monkeys. Perhaps we're still programmed to respond to a similar warning cry, from our early years as *Homo sapiens*.

Scary Celebrations

GHOULS. GHOSTS. SOULS OF THE DEAD. TO SOME, THEY MEAN A TIME TO SCREAM, RUN INSIDE, AND JUMP UNDER THE COVERS. BUT IN A NUMBER OF CULTURES AROUND THE WORLD, IT'S IMPORTANT TO CELEBRATE THE SOULS OF ONE'S ANCESTORS. INTERESTINGLY ENOUGH, WE OFTEN CELEBRATE THEM WITH FUN FOODS AND BIG MEALS—FUEL FOR THE LIVING.

Ghost Fest

Between the thirteenth and fifteenth day of the seventh lunar month of the Buddhist calendar, the Festival of the Dead is celebrated. On this day, ghosts and spirits emerge from the netherworld to visit the earth. The living (that's us) can make nice to the ghosts by offering special "spirit" money, and burying or releasing small paper boats and lanterns on the water, which give the ghosts "directions" to come and eat some treats. The climax of the celebration occurs when a priest tosses buns and candy to the ravenous ghosts. The crowds of children gathered usually rush up to eat the airborne sweets.

Halloween: Then

The name Halloween sounds like a sped-up version of "All Hallows' Evening," the eve before All Saints' Day on November 1st. Halloween's beginnings probably combined the fall feast of Hallowtide and an old Celtic festival called *Samhain* (pronounced sow-in), which celebrated the end of summer and the coming of winter. On October 31st, it was believed that the souls of the dead came back home to visit family. Food was left by doors to welcome the good spirits. Fires were lit to keep the evil spirits away, and scary masks were worn. This may explain some of the Halloween traditions we celebrate today in North America.

Halloween: Now

Modern-day Halloween began when Scottish and Irish immigrants brought their traditions to North America in the 1800s. For instance, the jack-o-lantern we know has its roots in Ireland, when turnips and rutabagas were carved up to ward off evil spirits. Trick-or-treating, which became popular in America between 1920 and 1950, likely has its beginnings in England. During All Souls' Day parades, poor people would come out to beg for food, and were given "soul cakes." Today, in North America, kids only have to use three magic words—"trick or treat"—to say that if they're not given candy, they'll perform a mischievous trick. But in Scotland, where it is known as guising, tricks must actually be performed in order to get the treats.

Day of the Dead

No, it's not the title of a zombie movie, but the name of a holiday held from October 31st to November 2nd in Mexico. On this day, parades are held in which people dressed as skeletons dance in the streets. It's a time for fun, but a time for reflection, as well. Families welcome the souls of the dead back into their homes, and go to visit and decorate relatives' graves. The graves serve as sites for picnics, and family members picnicking at nearby gravesites often mingle together. The meals are— excuse the pun—to die for, and include sugary desserts shaped in a number of animal and skull shapes and a special bread, *pan de muerto*, which means bread of the dead.

The Delight of Fright

By now, you've probably figured out how important fear is to us. It makes threats seem menacing, and lets us know when we need to worry about a situation. Fear fills our bodies with adrenaline and hormones that give us a rush of energy. When a dangerous situation isn't real, we can still get the same energy kick in a safe environment. Here's how.... Hold on!

Feel the Need for Speed!

A steel bar is lowered over your lap. The little cart you're sitting in inches—chug! chug!—up a steep hill. You reach the top and look down. The ground seems miles away. You hang there for a second, listening to your heart beat in your ears. Then...you're hurtling down the hill. The air is filled with screams. Roller coasters operate by two principles: 1) what goes up must come down (that's gravity), and 2) unless something stops it, an object in motion stays in motion (that's inertia). Many coasters have their biggest drops early on to build up energy for the rest of the ride. Although they are fast, most coasters use sharp turns to create the illusion of even greater speed, and the obstacles placed around the track heighten that sense of danger.

Gore Galore

If you think of theater, what comes to mind? Popcorn and a great action flick? How about a stage with spurting blood, acid throwing, eyeball gouging, scorpion stinging, and people being cut up into bits and pieces? Would you believe that this kind of grisly entertainment was one of the hottest tickets in Paris? It happened at a theater called the Grand Guignol (say *grahn geen-yol*), established back in 1897. The Grand Guignol specialized in plays that terrified audiences with their gory makeup effects. One theater director judged how successful a show was by the number of audience members who fainted. Although the theater closed in 1962, the term Grand Guignol is still used to describe entertainment with lots of (fake) blood and guts.

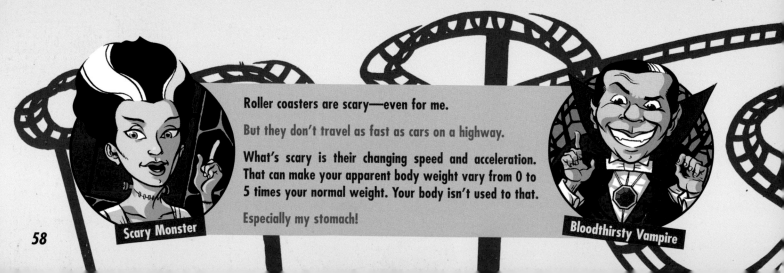

Roller coasters are scary—even for me.

But they don't travel as fast as cars on a highway.

What's scary is their changing speed and acceleration. That can make your apparent body weight vary from 0 to 5 times your normal weight. Your body isn't used to that.

Especially my stomach!

Scary Monster

Bloodthirsty Vampire

Coaster Conquerors

Have you always wanted to brave a roller coaster, but haven't had the courage? Psychologists from Harvard Medical School tested a program to help "coaster phobics." The program addressed the causes of a coaster phobia: height, speed and, especially, the feeling of being out of control. The program helped people learn to enjoy roller coasters by making them more comfortable with the sensations the rides create. For example, participants were asked to swing their heads around to create the dizzy feeling they'd have on a real ride. They also watched a movie of a roller coaster, and—ready?—they graduated by going to a theme park and getting on the real thing.

Lights, Camera... Shiver!

SCARY MOVIES GIVE AN AUDIENCE A BIG DOSE OF FEAR—IN A WAY THAT WON'T CAUSE REAL DANGER. THE MOVIEGOERS MAKE THEMSELVES VULNERABLE BY SITTING IN A DARK ROOM. THEN IT'S UP TO THE FILMMAKERS TO TURN ON THE SCARES.

Terror Train

Can you imagine paying to enter a movie theater, sitting down, and then watching a film entitled *Arrival of a Train at a Station*—a film that wouldn't even run one minute long? You'd probably yell at the manager and demand your money back. However, back on December 28th, 1895, few had seen a movie before, and certainly not one about a train pulling into a station. On that day, brothers Auguste and Louis Lumière invited a small crowd to the Grand Café in Paris to go down in history as the world's first paying movie audience. But did you know that they paid to see the world's first terror film? As the famous story goes, the audience members (who had never seen a movie before) were so shocked by the image of the approaching train that they got up from their seats in a panic to dodge it.

Get Hitched

One of the most influential film-makers of all time specialized in, as he put it, "playing the audience like a piano." Alfred Hitchcock's films play on our deepest fears, such as acrophobia, child abduction, and animal attacks. Hitchcock had numerous fears. A childhood incident caused him to distrust authority figures and confinement. After being bad, his father sent him to the police station with a note to lock him in a cell for five minutes. The memory of the traumatic event must have never left the famous director, who once admitted his greatest fear was of the police.

Scream, Wilhelm, Scream!

The scream, that piercing cry of terror, is the signature sound of fear. Scary movies are full of them. In 1951, a film called *Distant Drums* featured a character giving a notable loud shriek as an alligator ate him. The sound effect was later used for a character named Wilhelm in the 1953 movie *The Charge at Feather River*. In the 1970s, a sound designer tracked down that scream, named it after the character of Wilhelm, and put it into *Star Wars*. He loved the scream so much that he slotted it into every other *Star Wars* movie as well as the Indiana Jones series. To date, the effect has popped up in over 90 films over the years.

Tricky Schtick

In most horror movies, the scares stay on the screen—but this hasn't always been the case! One legendary producer in the 1950s and 60s used gimmicks that were even better than the films he made. William Castle gave audiences insurance policies for being scared to death, and passed out "ghost viewer" glasses at *13 Ghosts*, which allowed viewers to see eerie images during the movie. Castle also rigged theater seats with electric buzzers that would tingle audience members when the monster "escaped" into the theater in the appropriately named *The Tingler*. His movie *The House on Haunted Hill* used a technique Castle dubbed "Emergo." This simply meant that a plastic skeleton would "emerge" and rush at the screaming audience along a wire. Ooooh, scary stuff!

Fear This Movie!

Horror Tips for the Directors of Tomorrow

YOU'D THINK THAT MORE MONSTERS, MORE BLOOD, AND MORE ROARING CHAINSAWS WOULD MAKE FOR A SCARIER FILM, RIGHT? MAYBE A MESSIER FILM. REAL SCARES IN A MOVIE TAKE A MORE SUBTLE APPROACH. THE BIG TRICK IS IN THE PACING. TOO MANY GORY SCENES WILL LEAVE YOUR AUDIENCE FEELING NUMB. IF YOU SPEND TOO MUCH TIME BUILDING UP THE SUSPENSE BUT WITHOUT GIVING ANY GOOD SCARE MOMENTS, YOU MIGHT BORE THE AUDIENCE. HERE THEN ARE A FEW TIPS FOR FUTURE BUDDING HORROR FILMMAKERS.

Sounds Make Scares

You've just read about the power of screams on the previous page, so it's probably not a stretch to learn that sound is key in the horror film. Scary music can make a scene tense by cuing the audience that something bad will happen soon. So can taking the music away. Without music to cue the audience, they won't know what might happen next. Knowing when to keep a scene dead silent and when to shock the audience with a sudden, loud noise is one of the main tricks in horror filmmaking. Try using sounds that don't fit with the images. One horror movie created a terrifying effect by showing the image of a boy opening his mouth to cry, but substituting the sound for a cat's meowing screech.

Only Show a Little Bit of the Monster

This assumes your movie actually has a monster in it. The longer the audience gets to look at the monster, the less scary it will be. Only hinting at the monster, or showing a small part of it (like a shark's fin breaking the surface of the water) will cause the audience's excitable imagination to fill in the rest of the details in a scarier way than anything a filmmaker could achieve. If you do reveal your monster, put your actors in the background and have the monster leap up at the front of the screen. That quick scare will shock the audience silly!

Move the Camera...Slowly

Want to add some tension to your scene? Try letting the camera drift ever so slightly. Audiences feel as if something may happen...but they don't know what. You've just created suspense! Another neat trick is to tilt your camera on an angle to create an off-balance sensation. Film buffs call this a canted, or dutch, angle, which was used to the max in a famous thriller called *The Third Man*.

Lower the Lights

No big surprise here, especially if you've read the pages about fear of the dark. Light is what makes film and movies possible. By taking away the lights and pumping up the shadows, you trap not only your characters, but the entire audience, in darkness.

MOST IMPORTANT:

Remember to credit *Fear This Book* when you win your first Oscar! (Seriously. I'll even send you a thank-you note or something.)

Index